AF608376

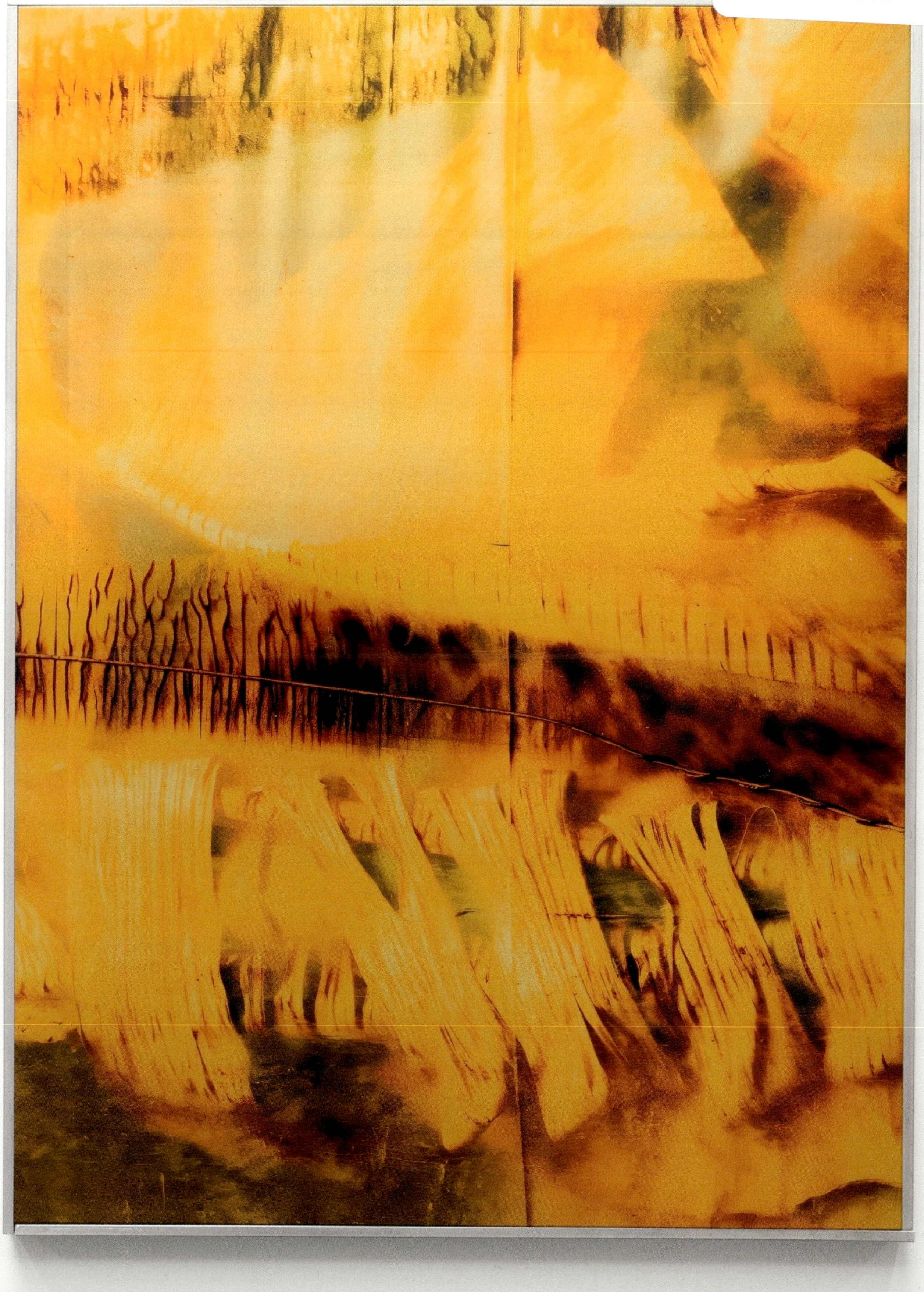

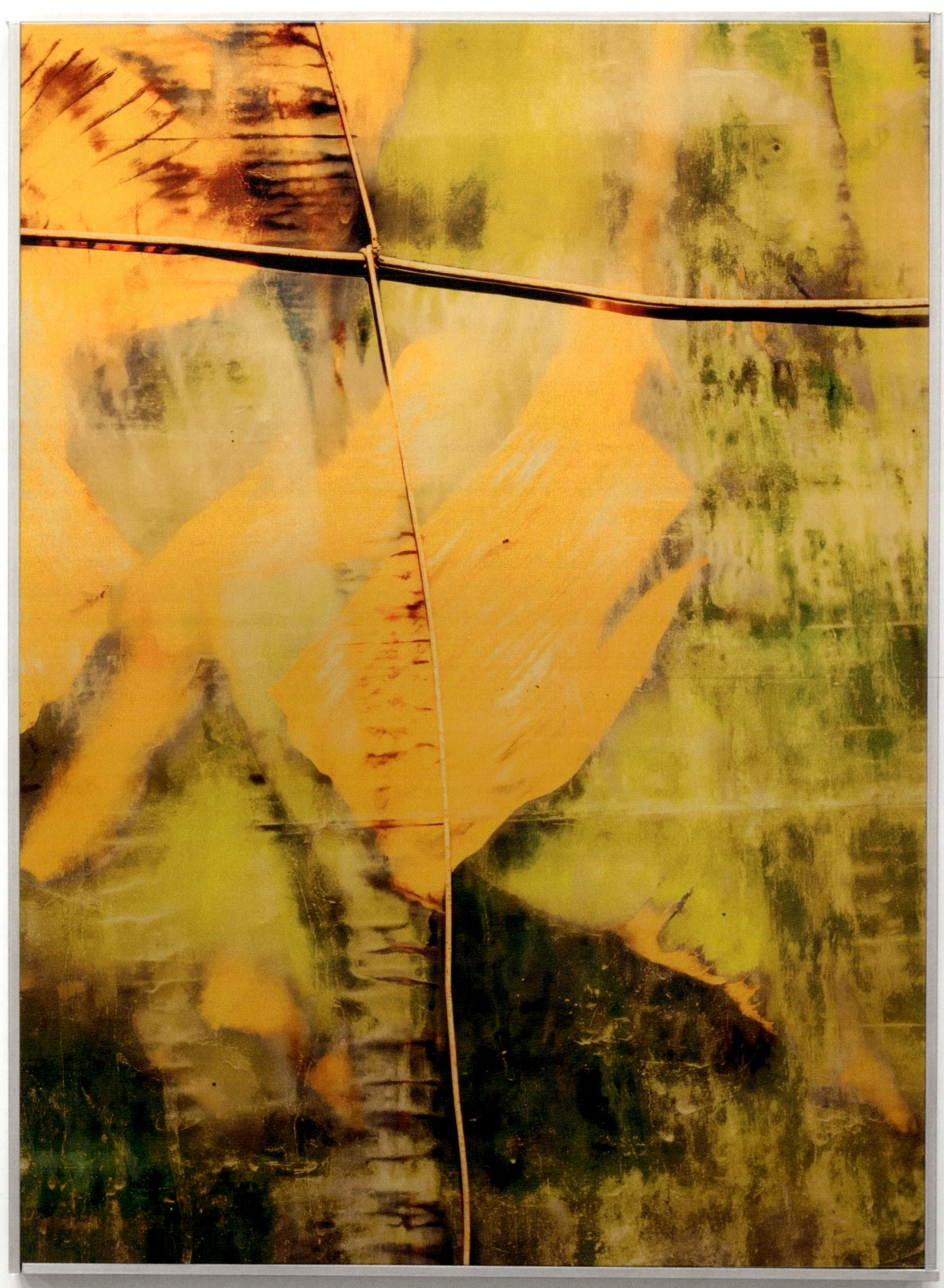

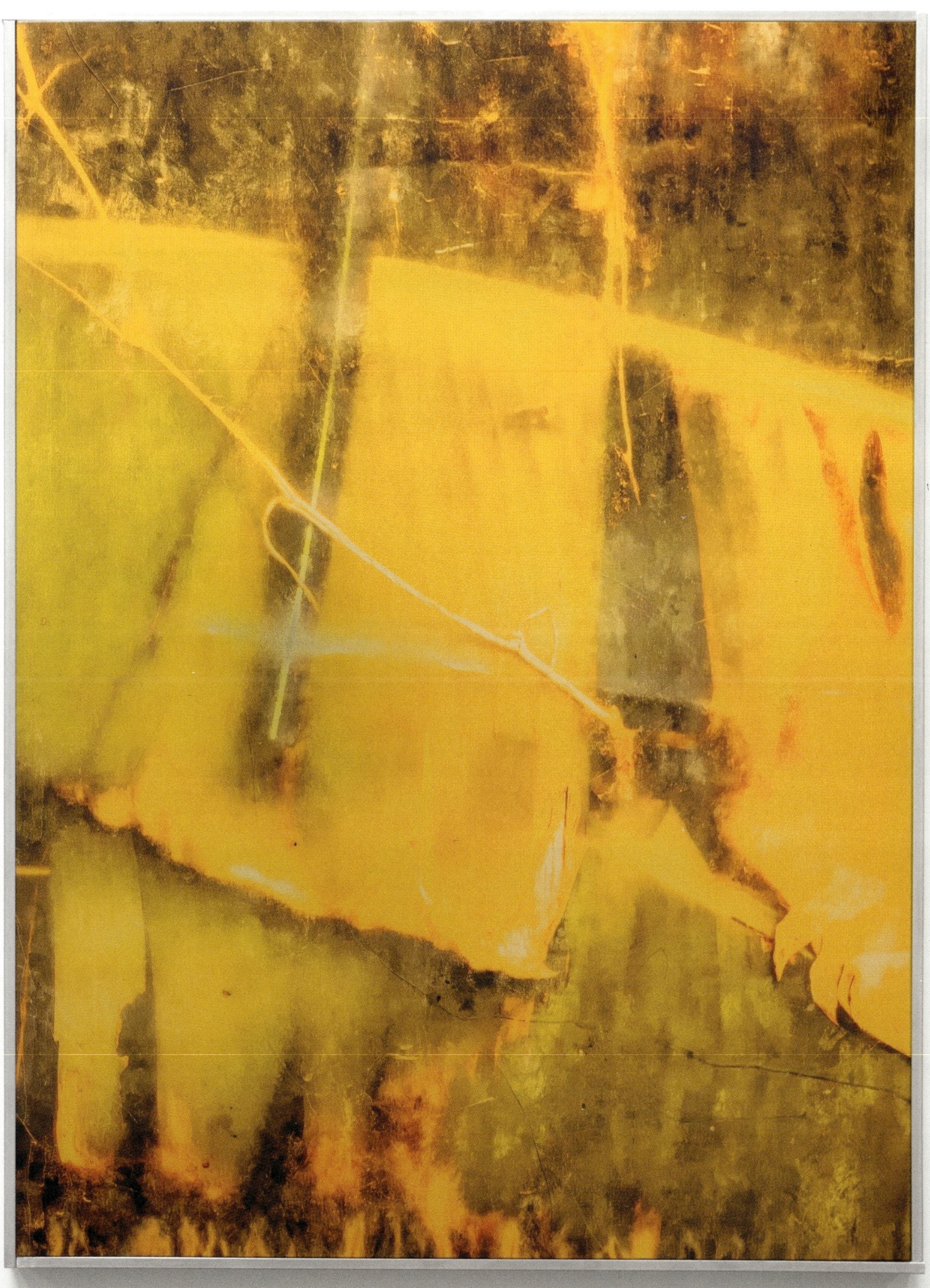

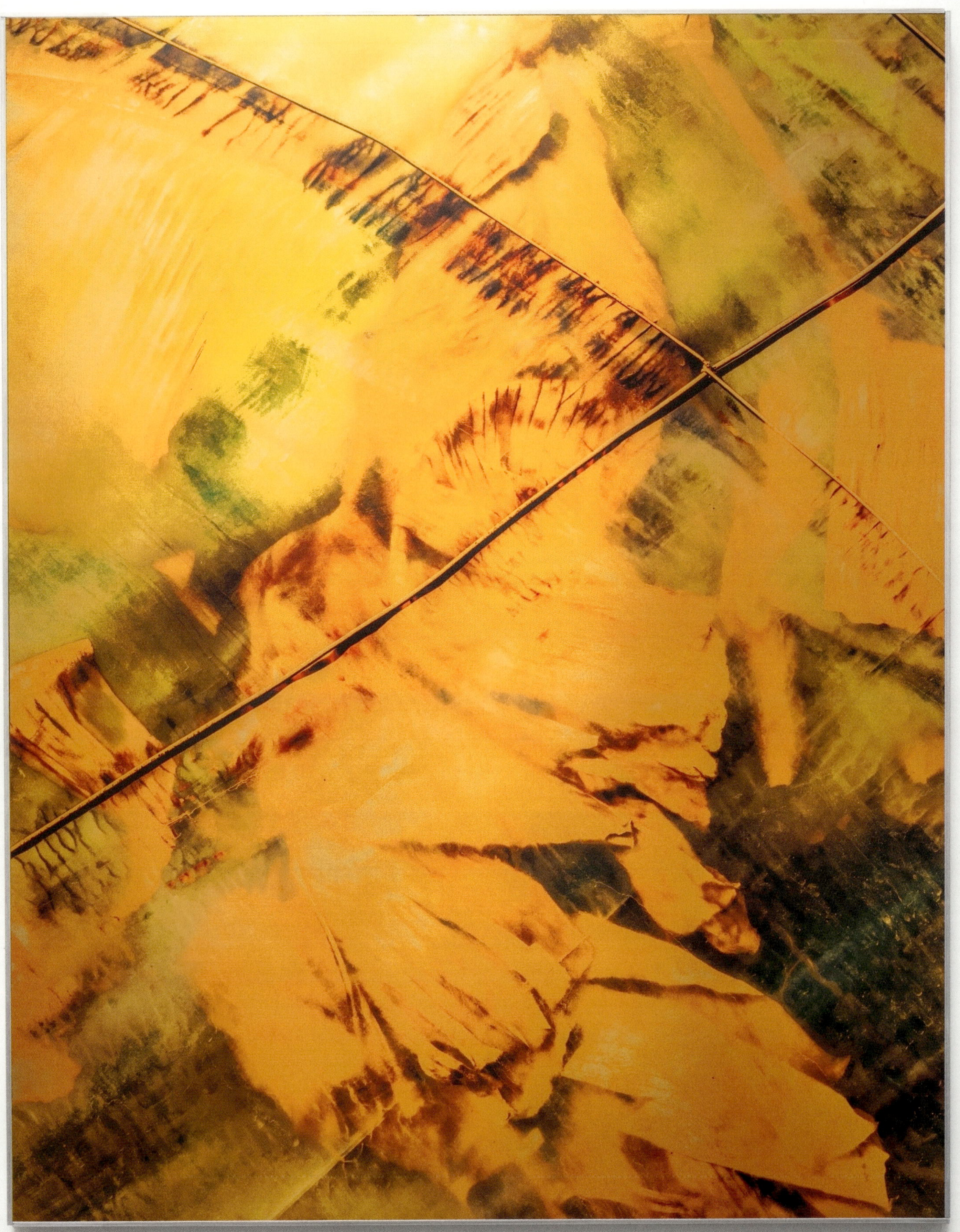

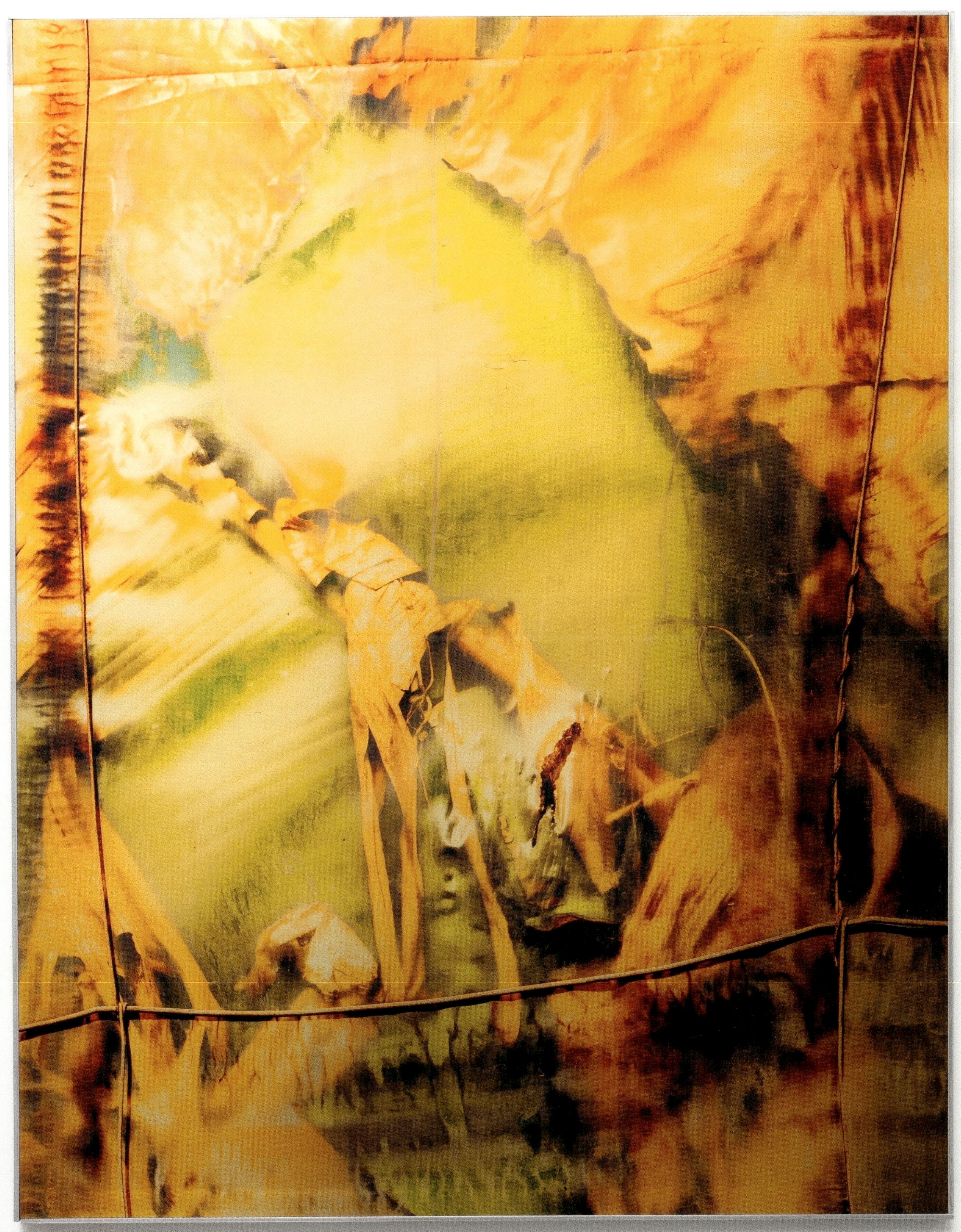

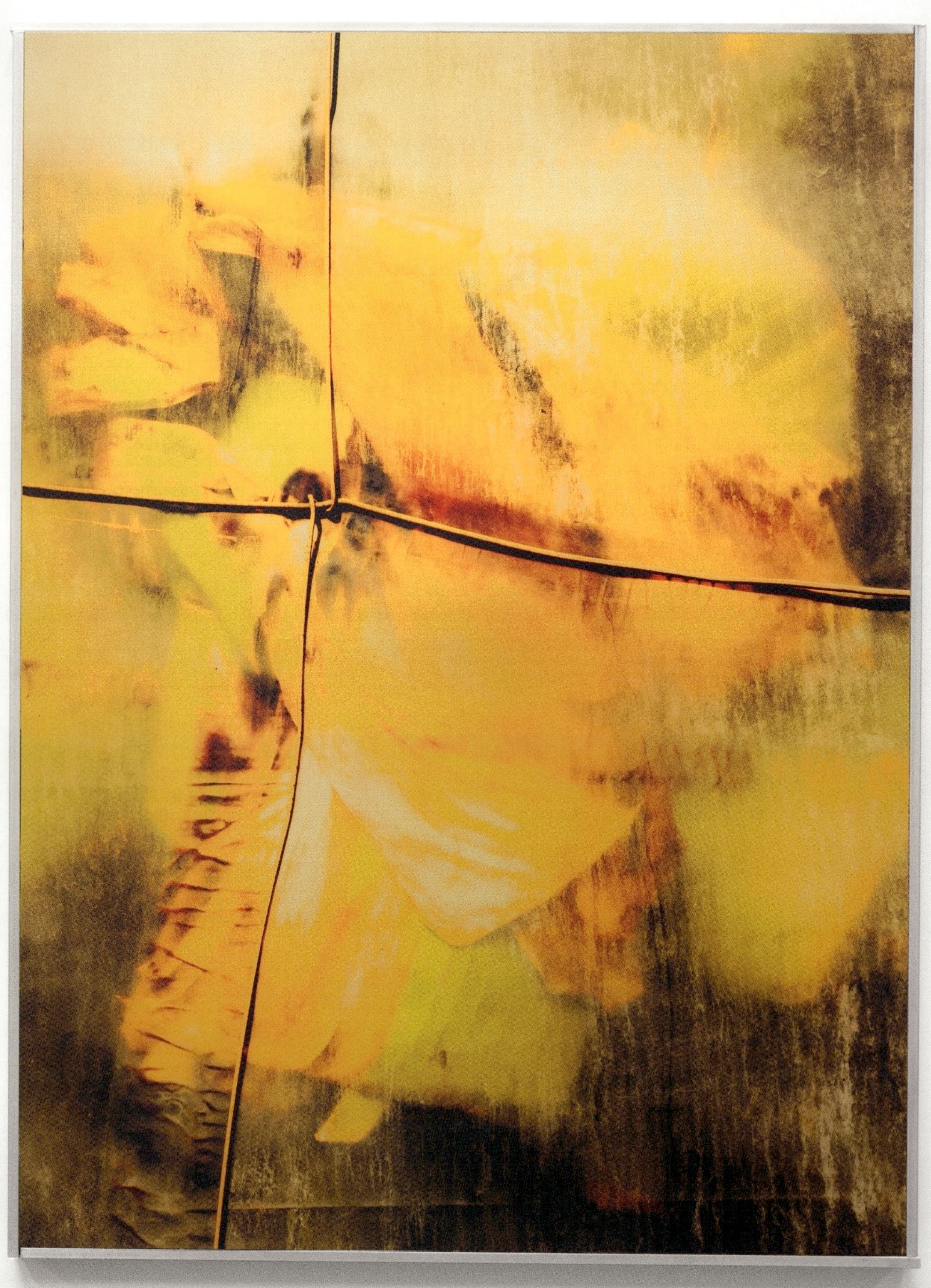

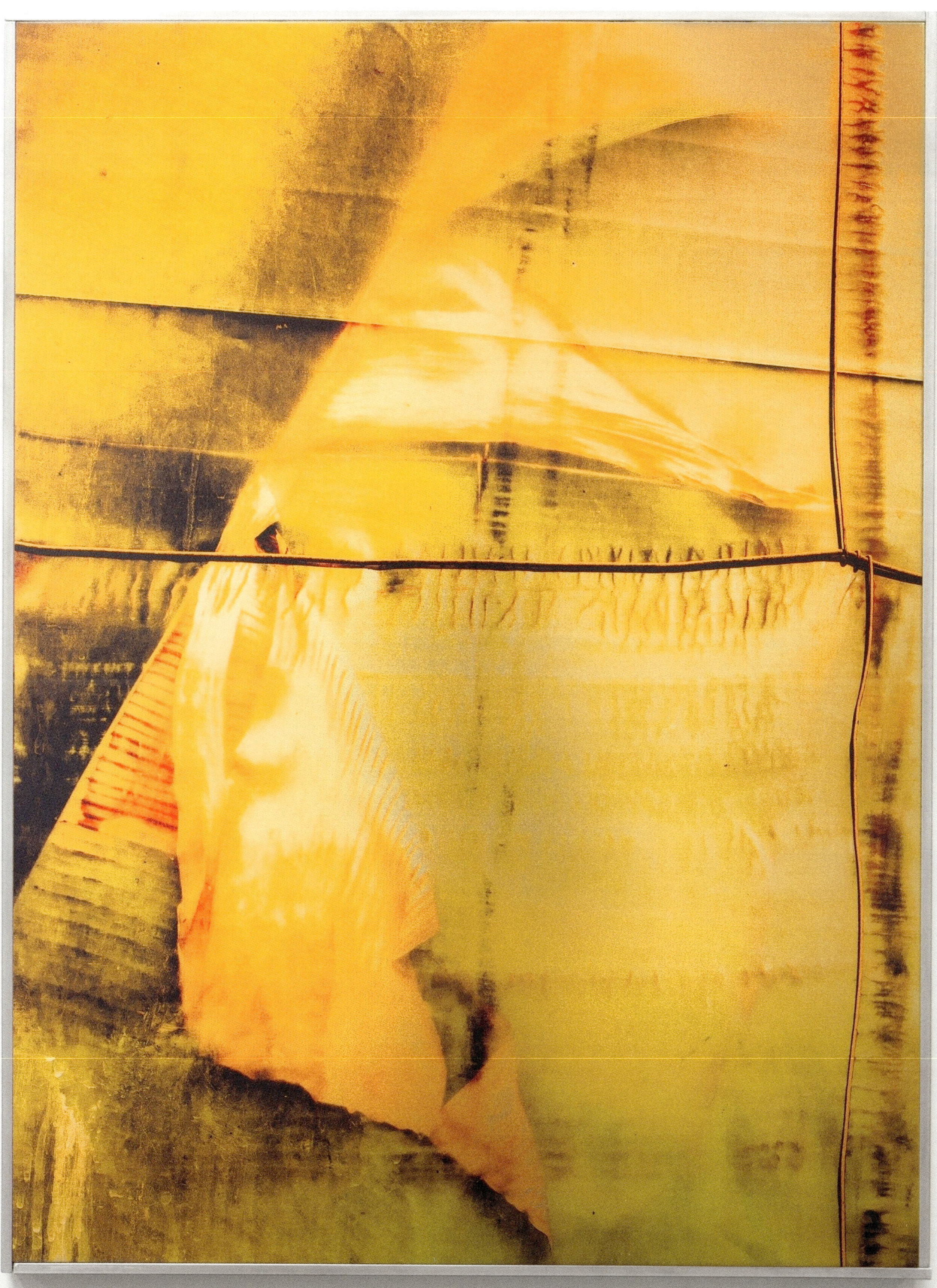

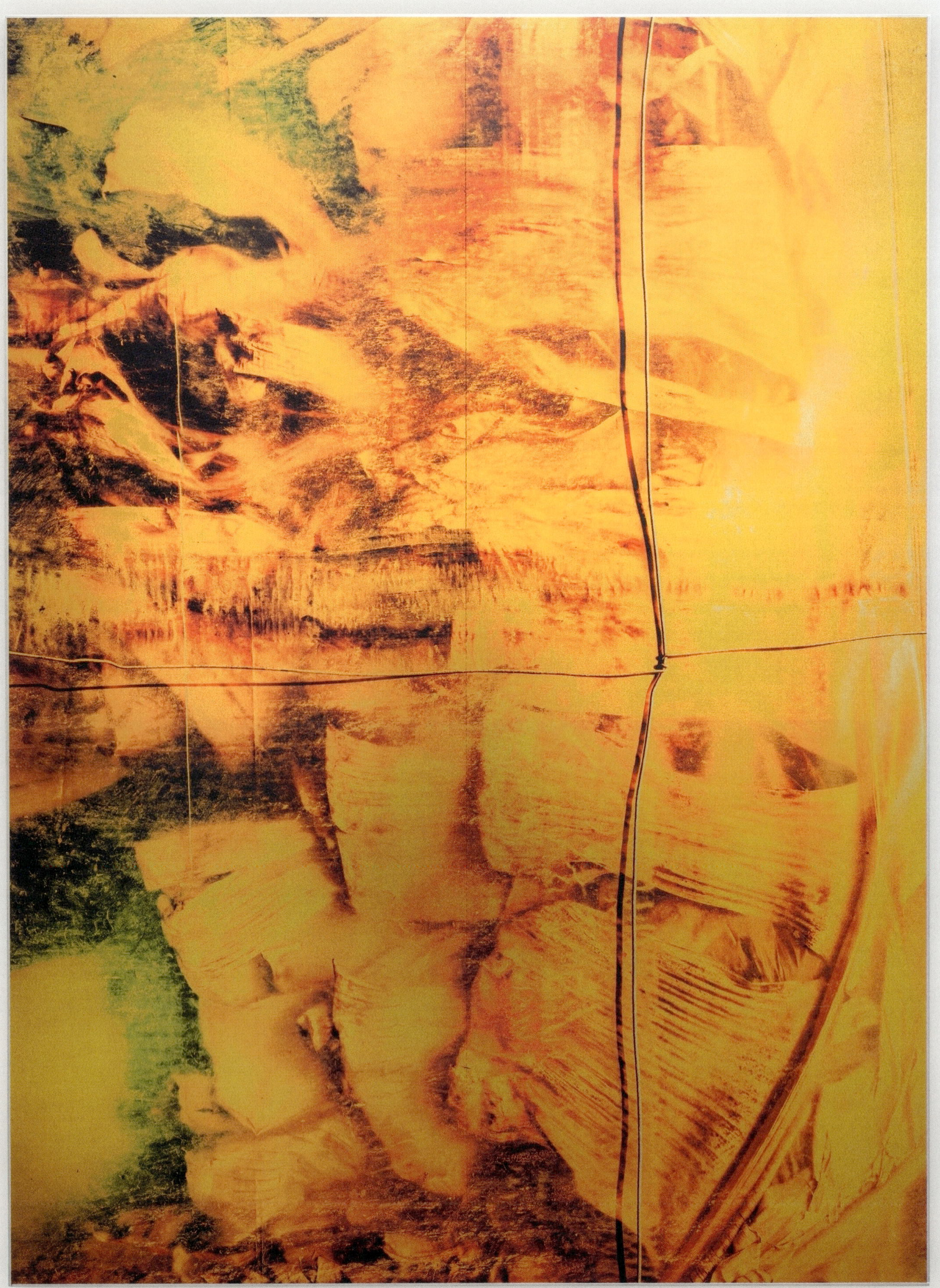

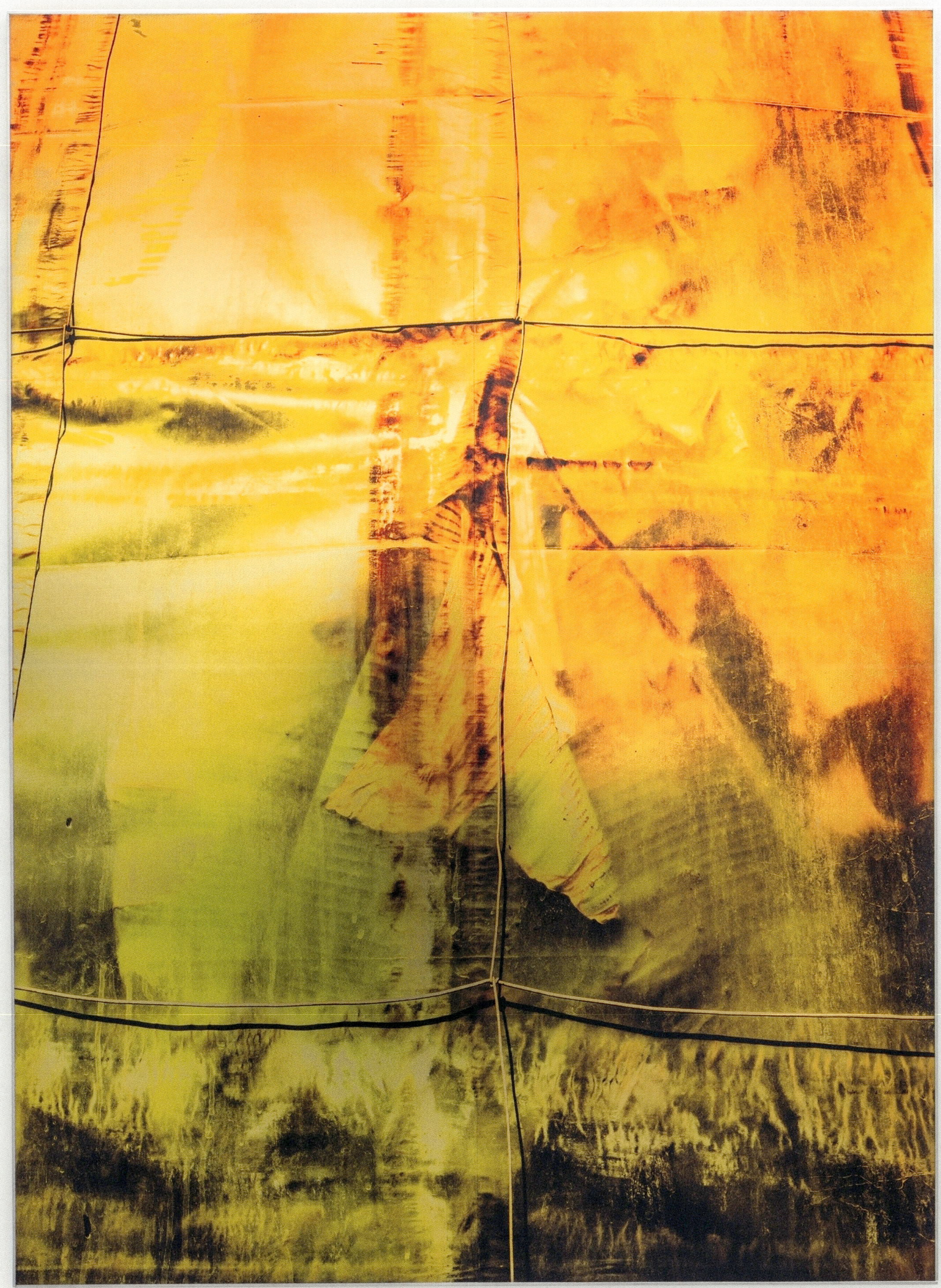

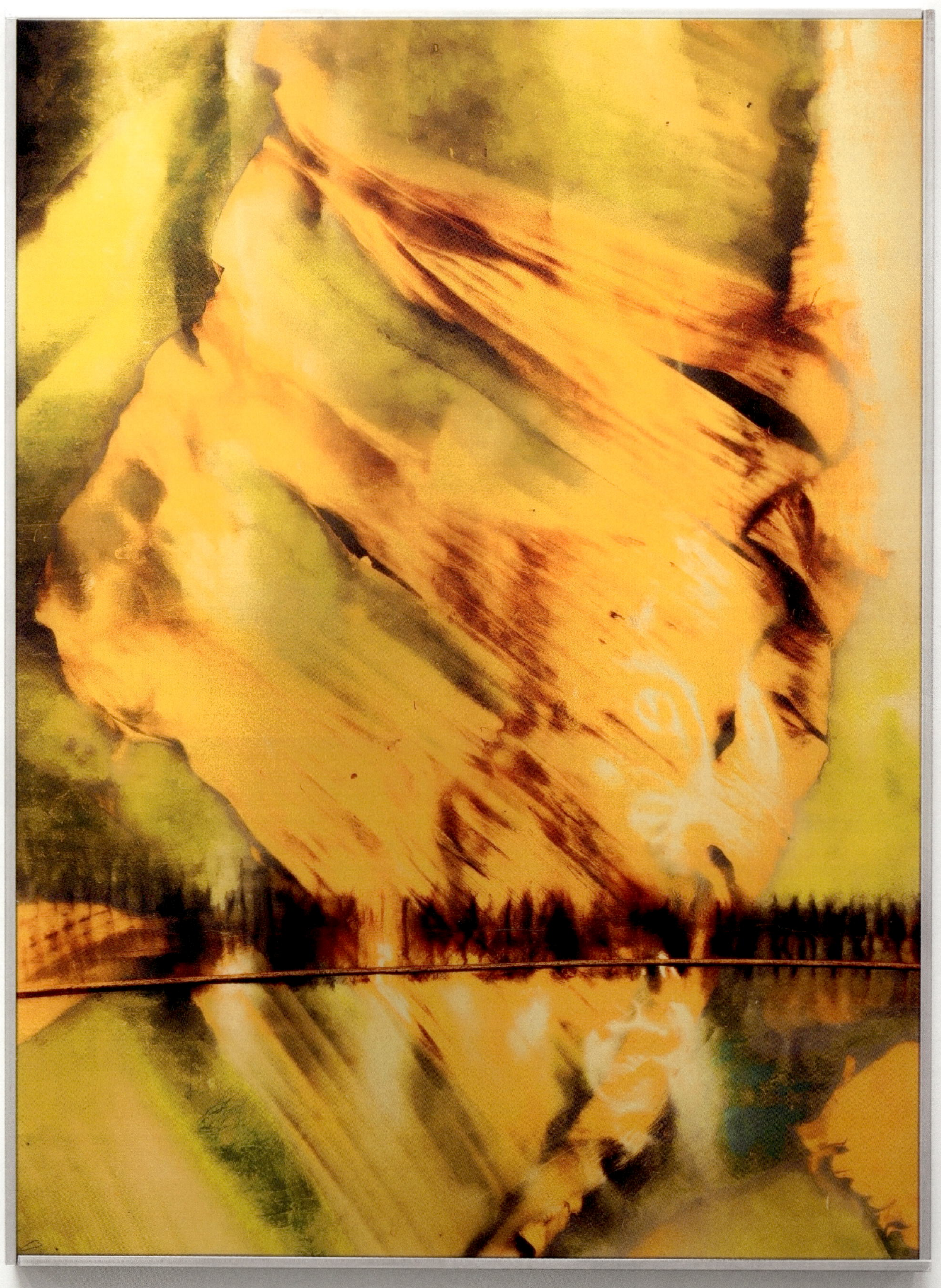

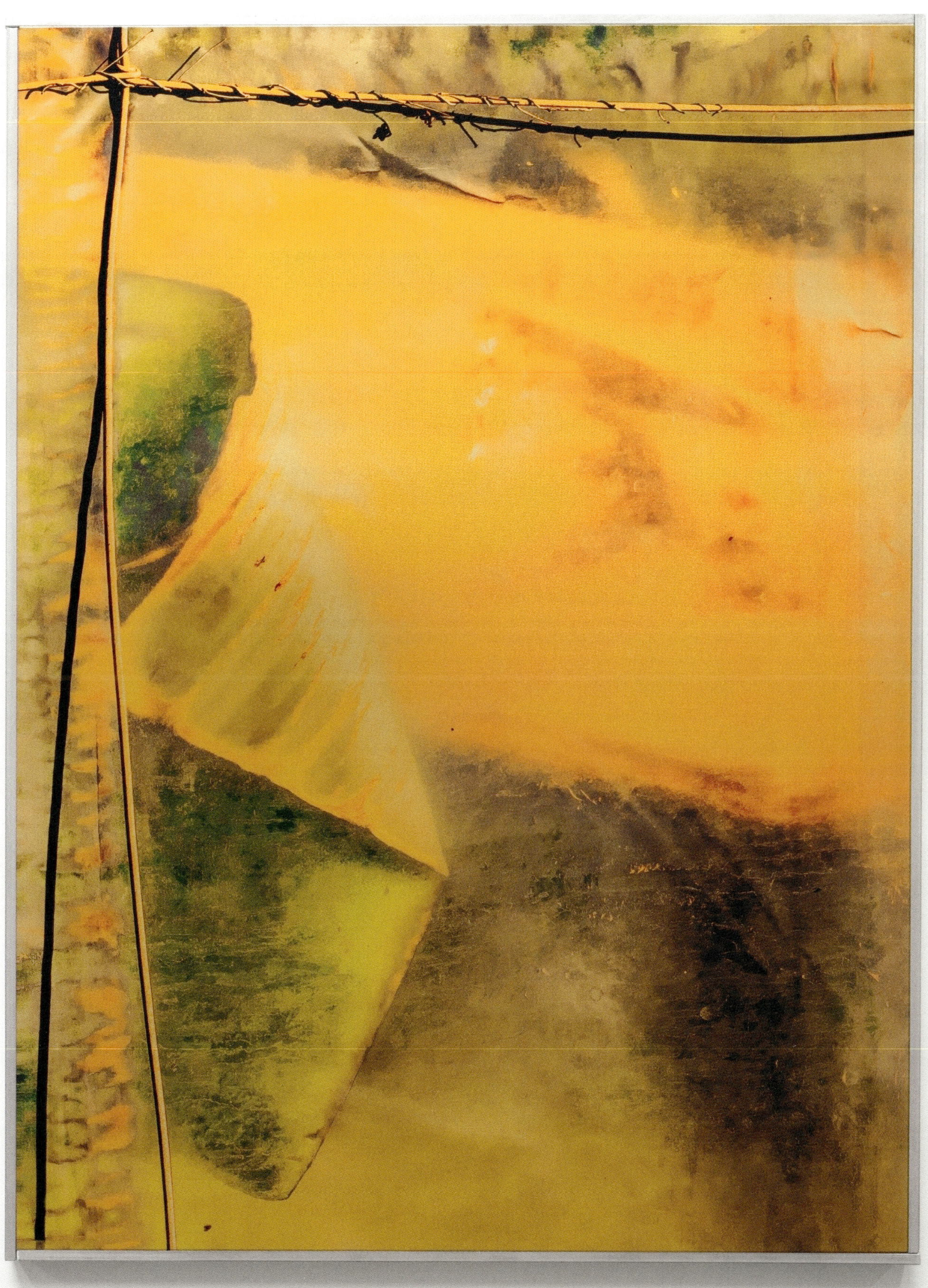

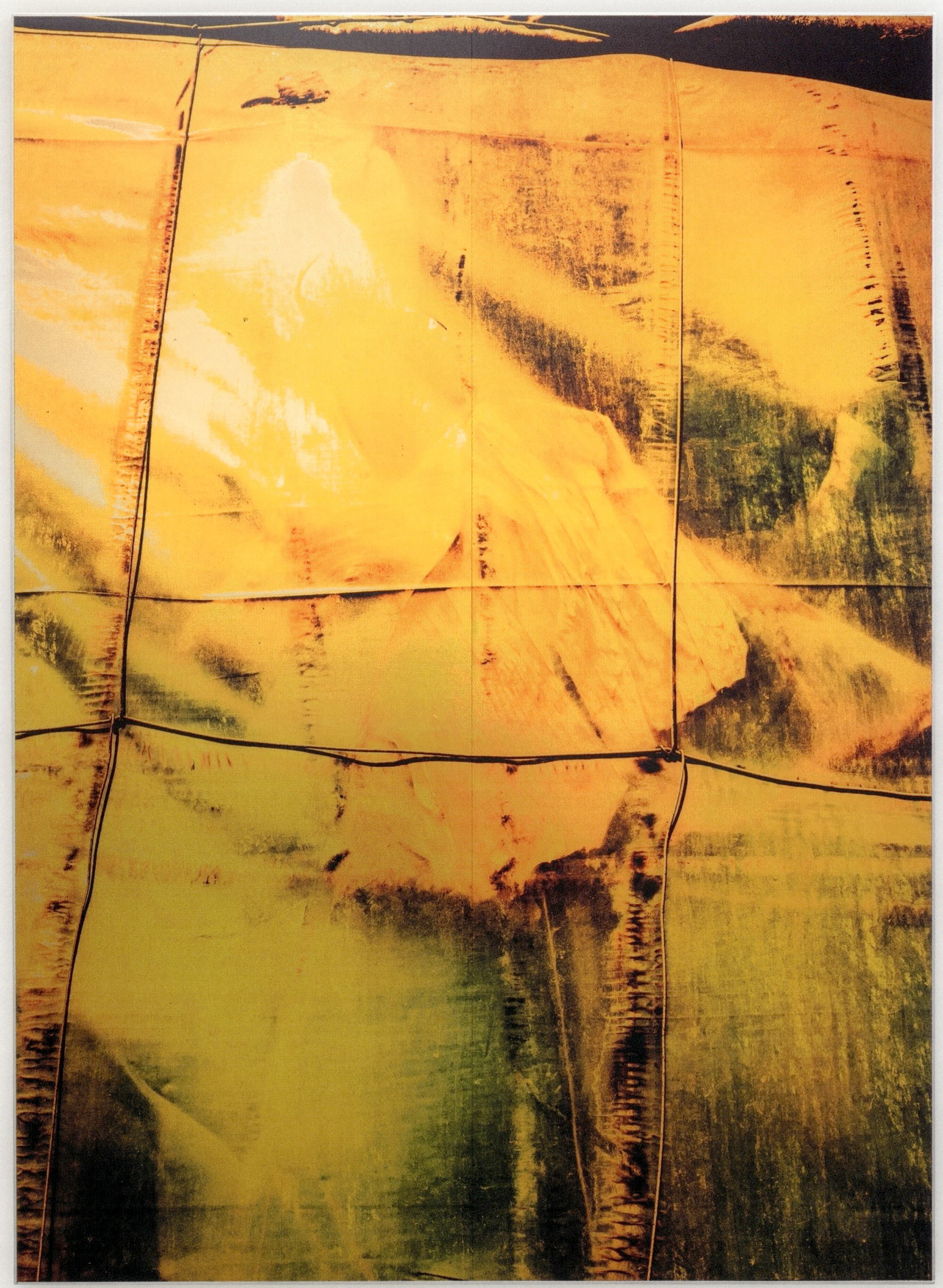

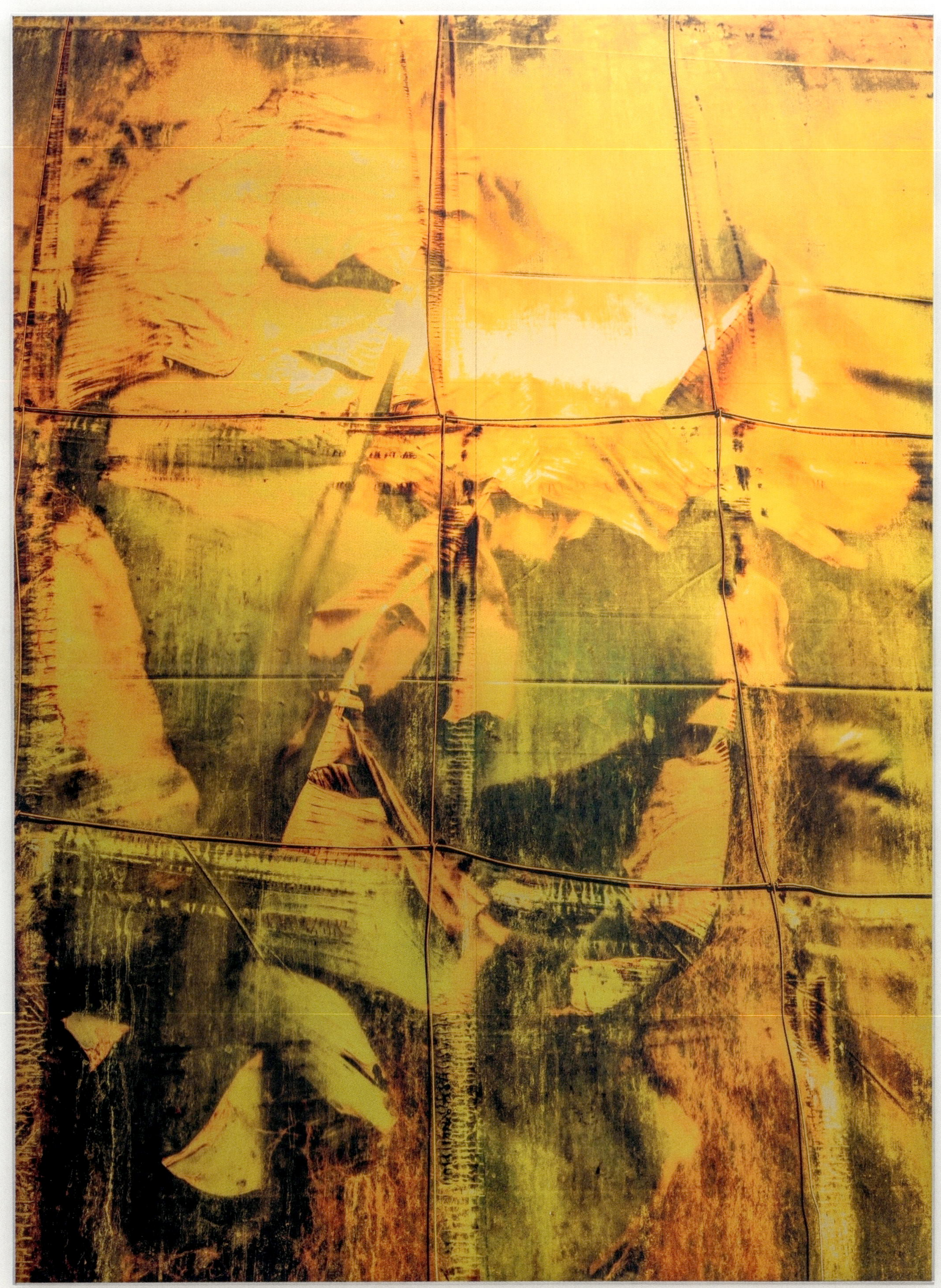

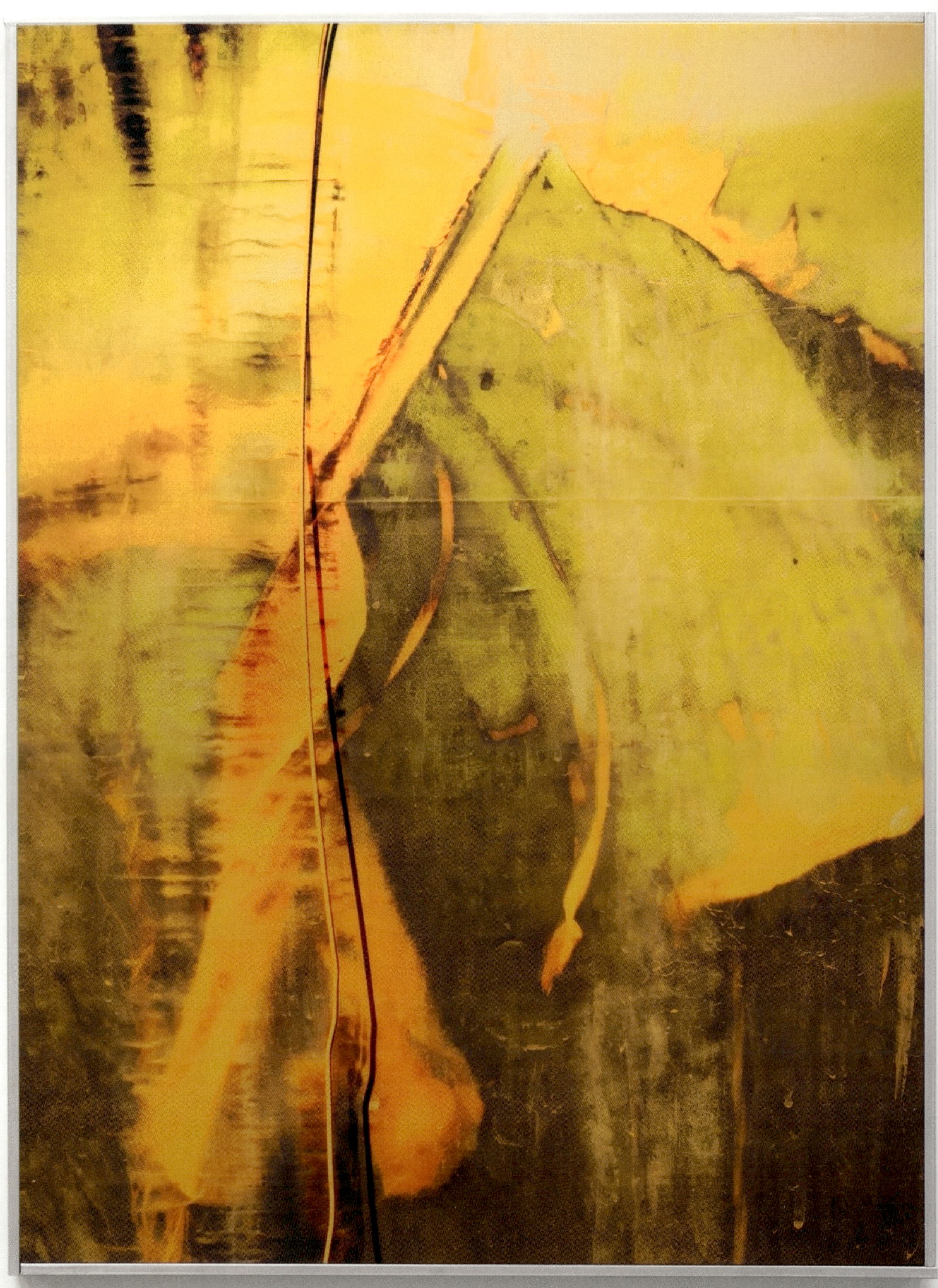

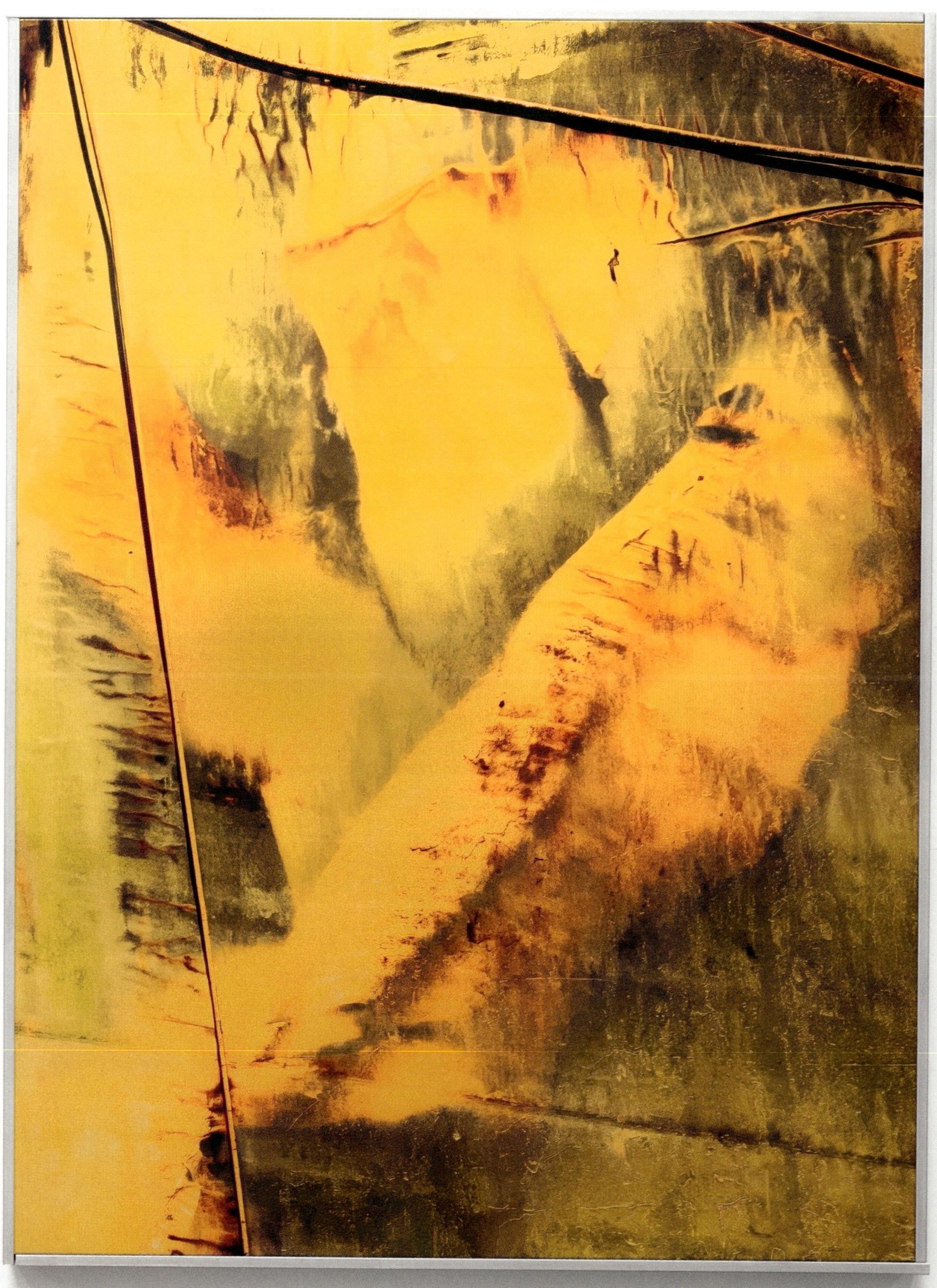

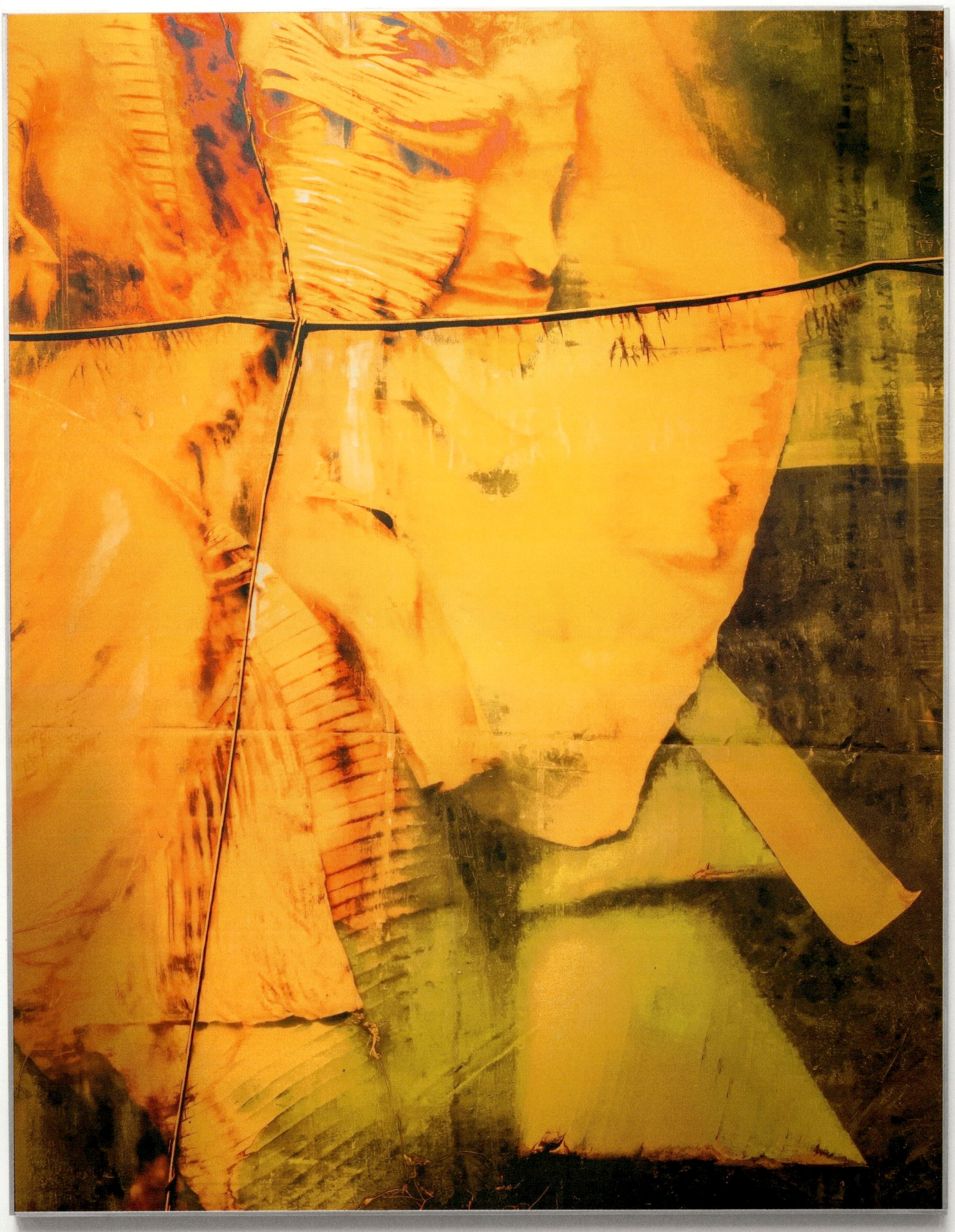

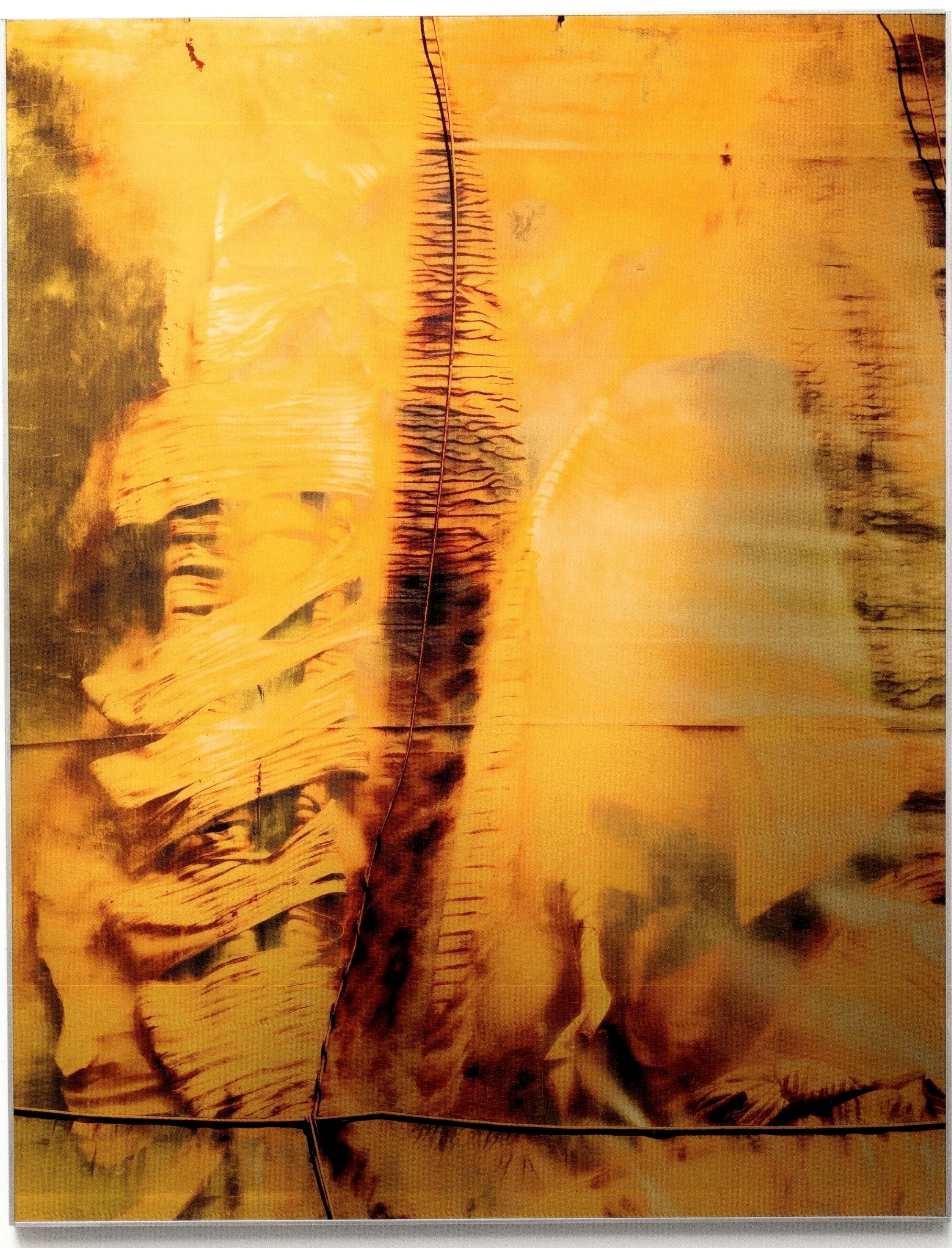

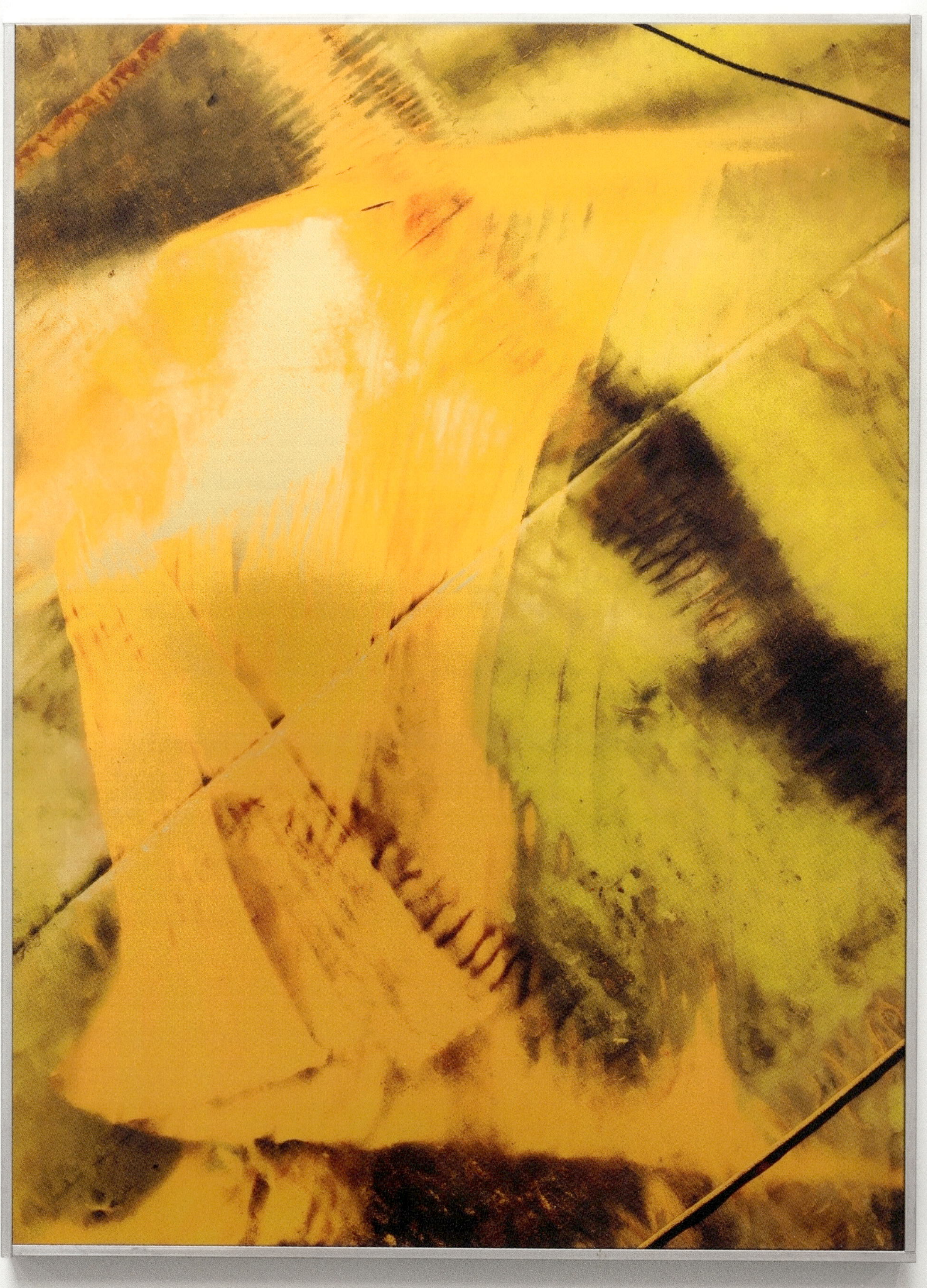

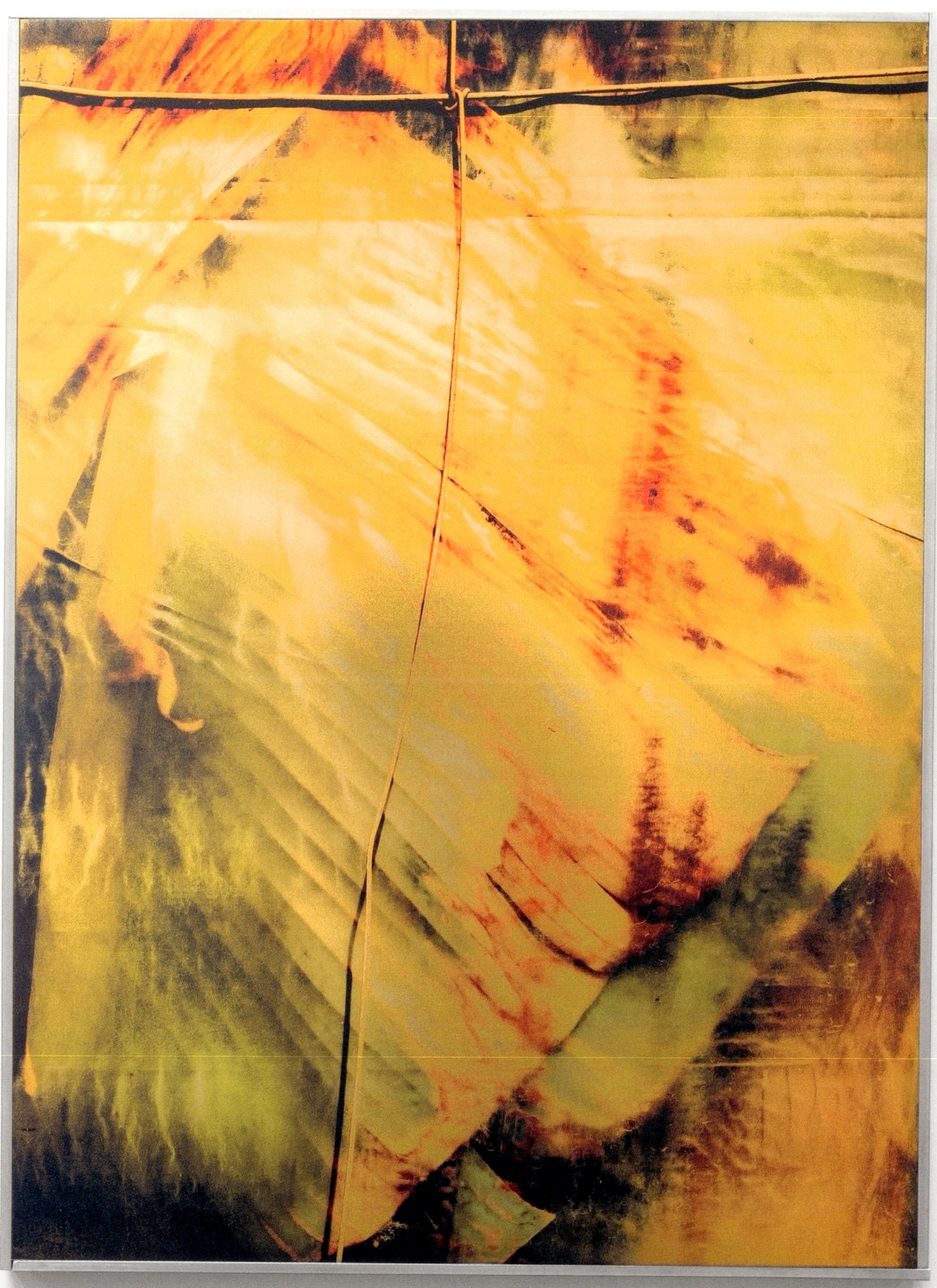

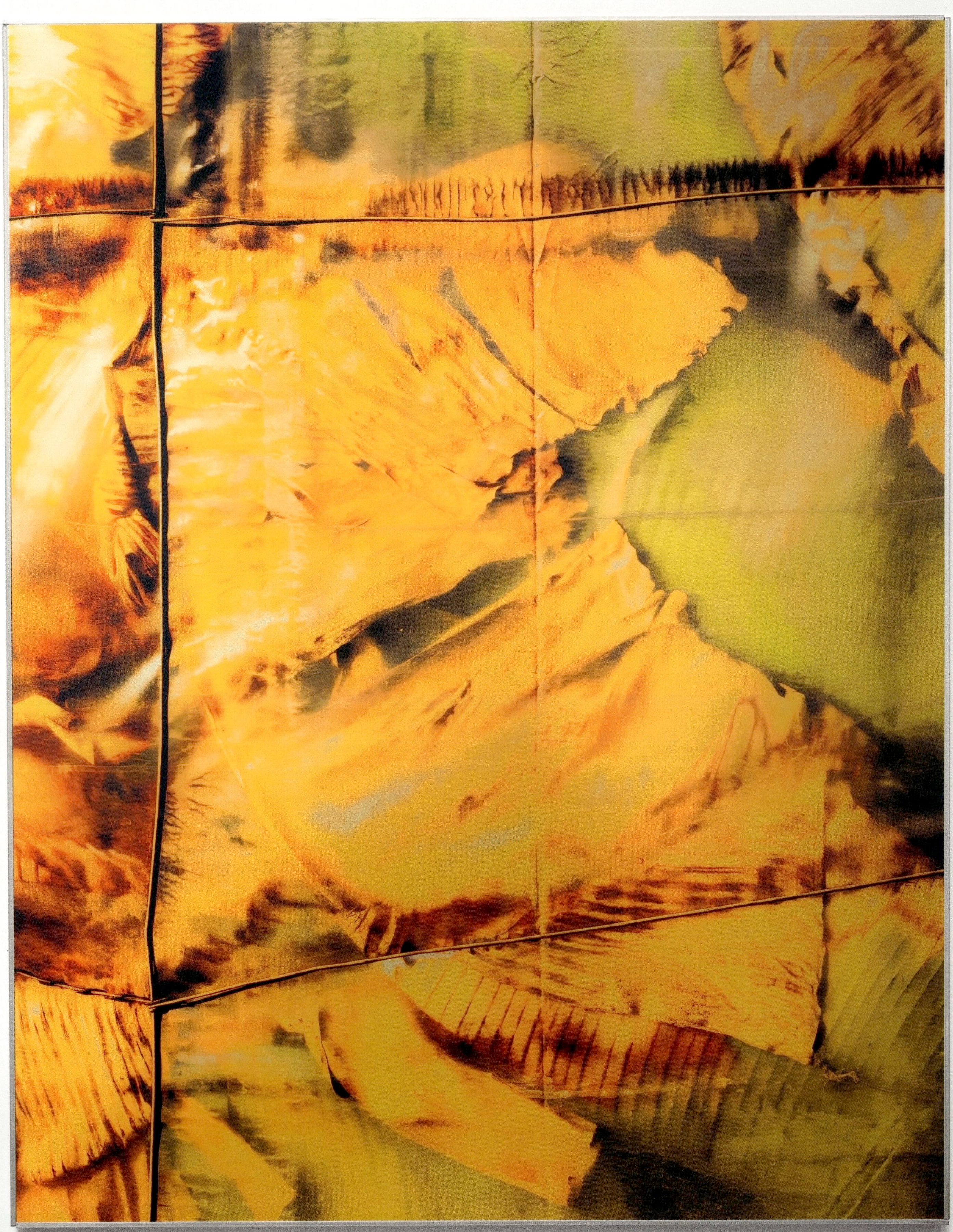

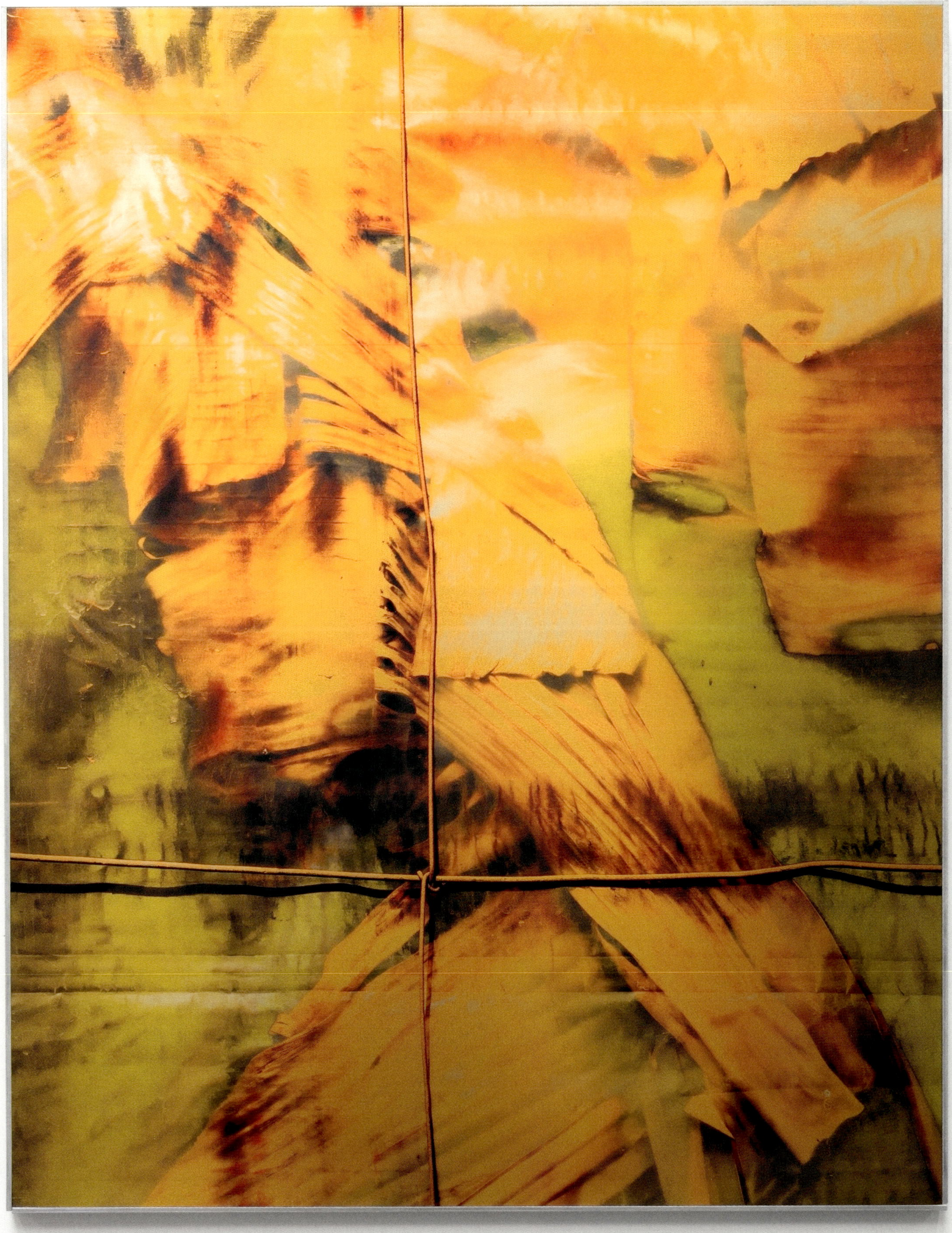

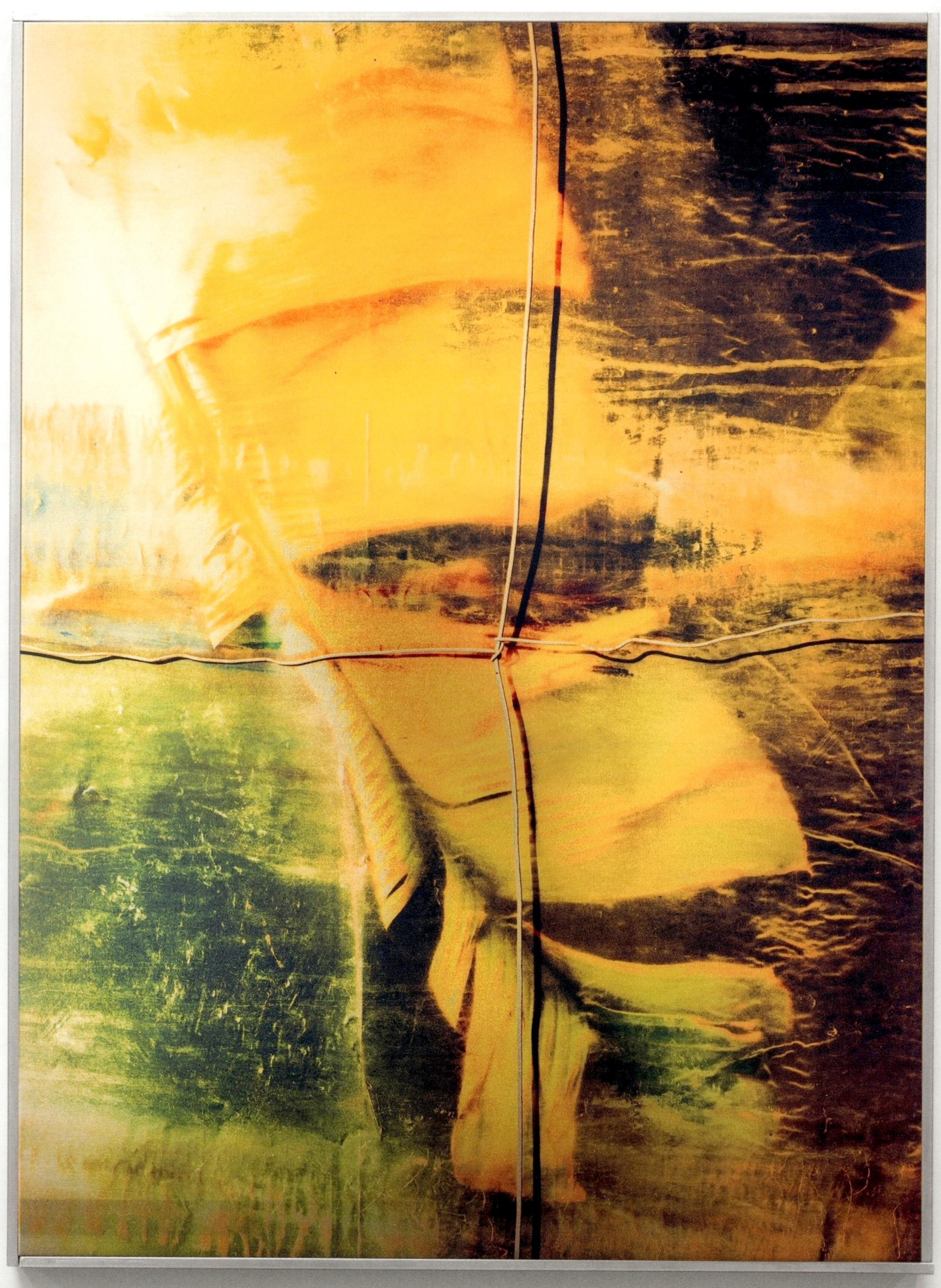

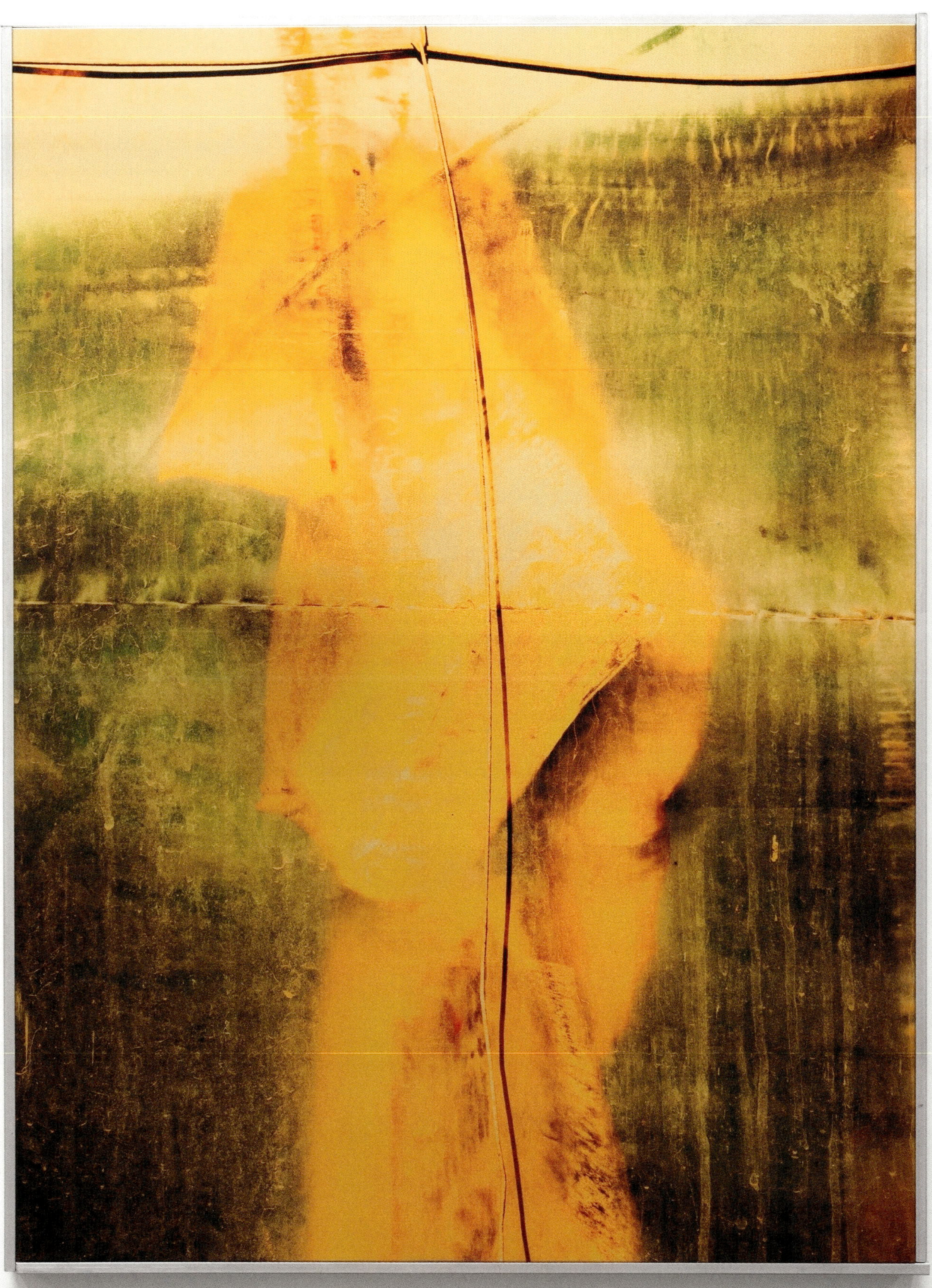

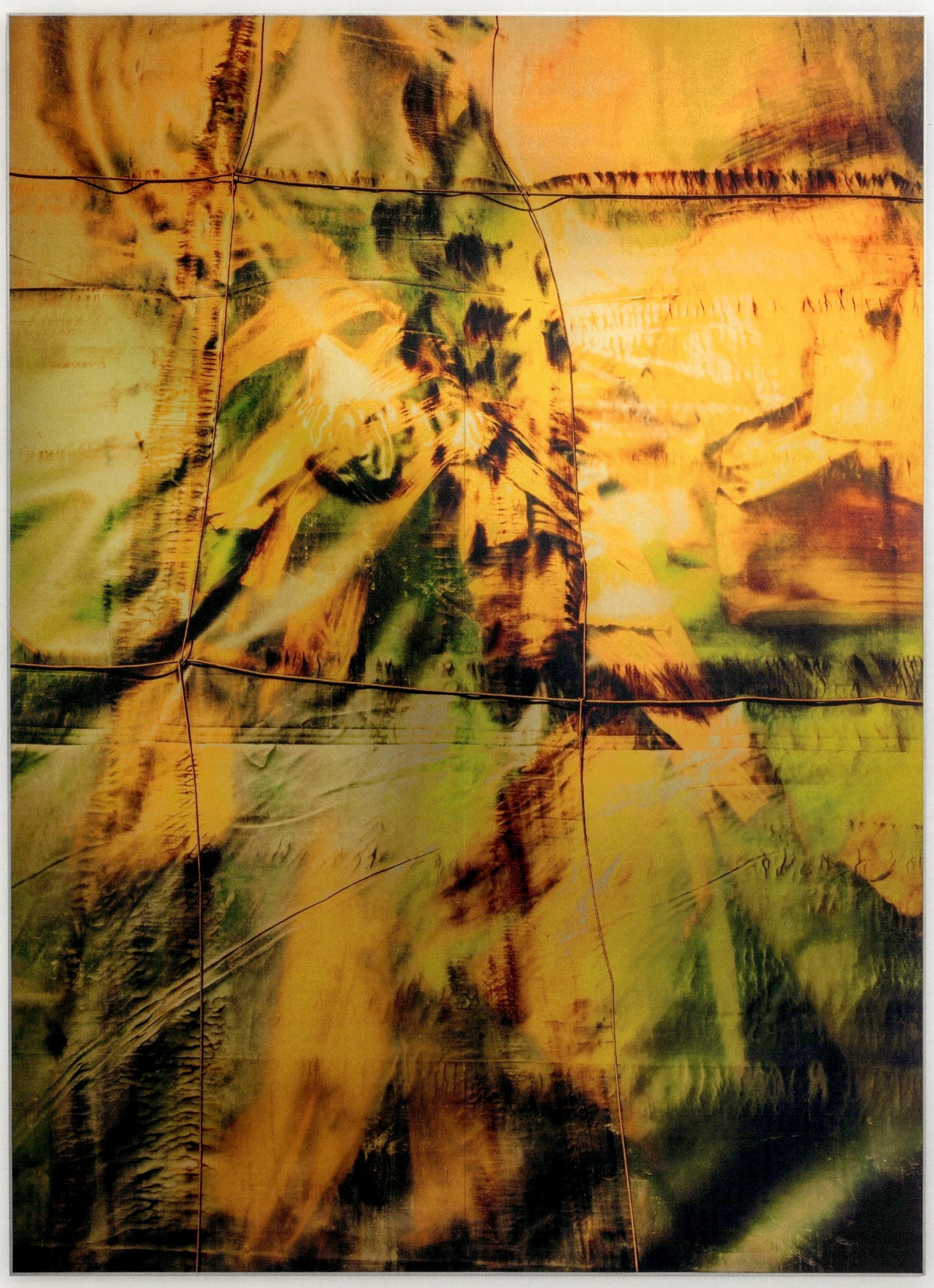

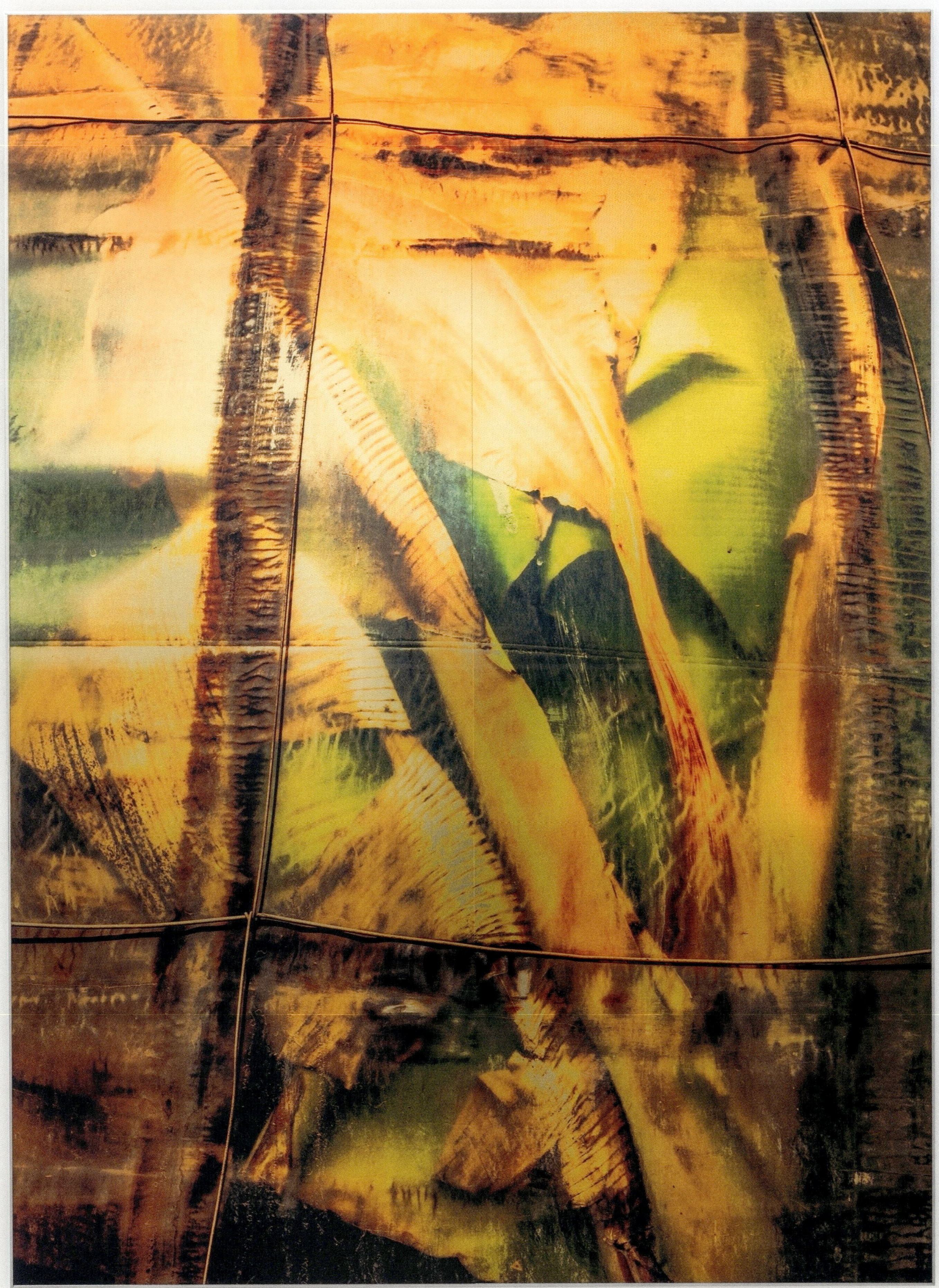

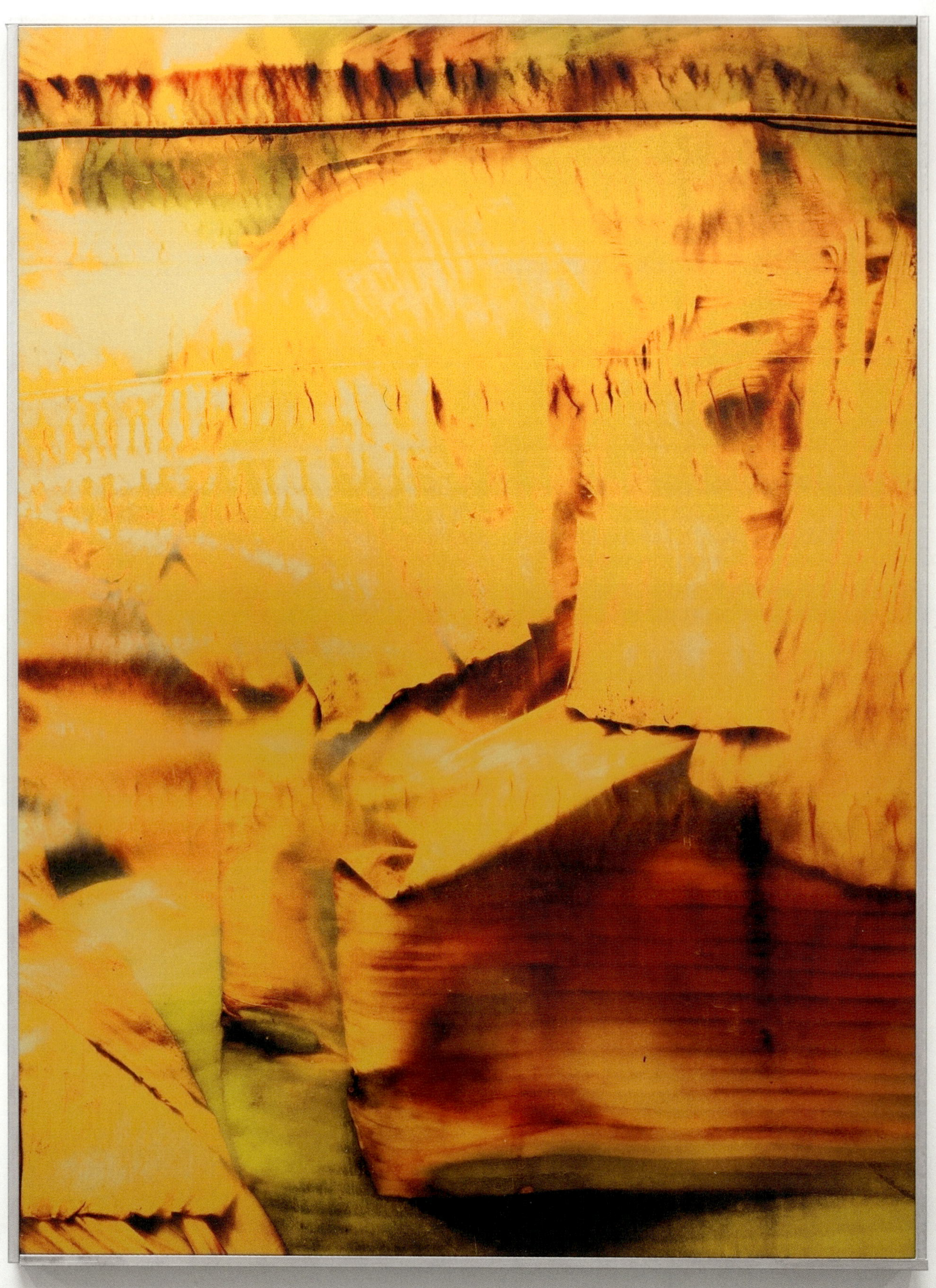

MUSA 15
38,5 x 51 x 2 CM , 2024
UV PRINT ON BRASS, VARNISH, STRETCHER BARS,
ALUMINIUM STRIPS, SCREWS

MUSA 09
38,5 x 51 x 2 CM, 2024
UV PRINT ON BRASS, VARNISH, STRETCHER BARS,
ALUMINIUM STRIPS, SCREWS

MUSA 17
38,5 x 51 x 2 CM, 2024
UV PRINT ON BRASS, VARNISH, STRETCHER BARS,
ALUMINIUM STRIPS, SCREWS

MUSA 22
101 x 81 x 2 CM, 2024
UV PRINT ON BRASS, VARNISH, STRETCHER BARS,
ALUMINIUM STRIPS, SCREWS

MUSA 19
101 x 81 x 2 CM, 2024
UV PRINT ON BRASS, VARNISH, STRETCHER BARS,
ALUMINIUM STRIPS, SCREWS

MUSA 07
38,5 x 51 x 2 CM, 2024
UV PRINT ON BRASS, VARNISH, STRETCHER BARS,
ALUMINIUM STRIPS, SCREWS

MUSA 04
38,5 x 51 x 2 CM, 2024
UV PRINT ON BRASS, VARNISH, STRETCHER BARS,
ALUMINIUM STRIPS, SCREWS

MUSA 26
151 x 201 x 2 CM, 2024
UV PRINT ON BRASS, VARNISH, STRETCHER BARS,
ALUMINIUM STRIPS, SCREWS

MUSA 01
151 x 201 x 2 CM, 2024
UV PRINT ON BRASS, VARNISH, STRETCHER BARS,
ALUMINIUM STRIPS, SCREWS

MUSA 10
38,5 x 51 x 2 CM, 2024
UV PRINT ON BRASS, VARNISH, STRETCHER BARS,
ALUMINIUM STRIPS, SCREWS

MUSA 12
38,5 x 51 x 2 CM, 2024
UV PRINT ON BRASS, VARNISH, STRETCHER BARS,
ALUMINIUM STRIPS, SCREWS

MUSA 25
151 x 201 x 2 CM, 2024
UV PRINT ON BRASS, VARNISH, STRETCHER BARS,
ALUMINIUM STRIPS, SCREWS

MUSA 24
151 x 201 x 2 CM, 2024
UV PRINT ON BRASS, VARNISH, STRETCHER BARS,
ALUMINIUM STRIPS, SCREWS

MUSA 16
38,5 x 51 x 2 CM, 2024
UV PRINT ON BRASS, VARNISH, STRETCHER BARS,
ALUMINIUM STRIPS, SCREWS

MUSA 14
38,5 x 51 x 2 CM, 2024
UV PRINT ON BRASS, VARNISH, STRETCHER BARS,
ALUMINIUM STRIPS, SCREWS

MUSA 23
101 x 81 x 2 CM, 2024
UV PRINT ON BRASS, VARNISH, STRETCHER BARS,
ALUMINIUM STRIPS, SCREWS

MUSA 21
101 x 81 x 2 CM 2024
UV PRINT ON BRASS, VARNISH, STRETCHER BARS,
ALUMINIUM STRIPS, SCREWS

MUSA 13
38,5 x 51 x 2 CM 2024
UV PRINT ON BRASS, VARNISH, STRETCHER BARS,
ALUMINIUM STRIPS, SCREWS

MUSA 06
38,5 x 51 x 2 CM 2024
UV PRINT ON BRASS, VARNISH, STRETCHER BARS,
ALUMINIUM STRIPS, SCREWS

MUSA 20
101 x 81 x 2 CM 2024
UV PRINT ON BRASS, VARNISH, STRETCHER BARS,
ALUMINIUM STRIPS, SCREWS

MUSA 18
101 x 81 x 2 CM, 2024
UV PRINT ON BRASS, VARNISH, STRETCHER BARS,
ALUMINIUM STRIPS, SCREWS

MUSA 05
38,5 x 51 x 2 CM, 2024
UV PRINT ON BRASS, VARNISH, STRETCHER BARS,
ALUMINIUM STRIPS, SCREWS

MUSA 11
38,5 x 51 x 2 CM, 2024
UV PRINT ON BRASS, VARNISH, STRETCHER BARS,
ALUMINIUM STRIPS, SCREWS

MUSA 03
151 x 201 x 2 CM, 2024
UV PRINT ON BRASS, VARNISH, STRETCHER BARS,
ALUMINIUM STRIPS, SCREWS

MUSA 02
151 x 201 x 2 CM, 2024
UV PRINT ON BRASS, VARNISH, STRETCHER BARS,
ALUMINIUM STRIPS, SCREWS

MUSA 08
38,5 x 51 x 2 CM, 2024
UV PRINT ON BRASS, VARNISH, STRETCHER BARS,
ALUMINIUM STRIPS, SCREW

APE#235

ISBN 9789083438436

www.artpapereditions.org
www.sybrenvanoverberghe.com

September 2024

Graphic Design:
Jurgen Maelfeyt

Courtesy of Keteleer Gallery